The NO BARKING at the TABLE!

C O O K B O O K

Wendy Boyd-Smith

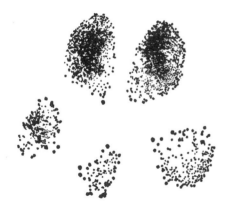

Webster

The NO BARKING at the TABLE!
COOKBOOK

by Wendy Boyd-Smith

Illustrations by Barney Saltzberg

Lip Smackers, Inc.

Lip Smackers, Inc.
P. O. Box 5385
Culver City, CA 90231-5385

Library of Congress Cataloging in Publication Data

Boyd-Smith, Wendy
    The No Barking at the Table Cookbook / Wendy Boyd-Smith

ISBN 9780962945908

Includes index
        1. cooking 2. dogs 3. title

Illustrations by Barney Saltzberg
Cover design by Heidi Frieder
Art Direction by Bethann Wetzel

Printed in the United States of America by
        Eerdmans
        Tallahassee, Florida

Reprinted, December 1991

I dedicate this book to my Mom and Dad, Alan & Melinda Blinken, for their love and support and their foresight in encouraging me to continue my education despite my being dyslexic. Their belief that I am a special person has enabled me to do anything I set my heart on and helped me to create and achieve my goals.

Thank you with all my love,

Wendy

*I dedicate these drawings to Miranda,
a true gourmutt!*

Barney

ACKNOWLEDGEMENTS

It is not possible to give thanks to all those responsible for helping me achieve one of my dreams.

This project would have been impossible without the help and support of my husband Tim, whose patience is everlasting. My thanks to Bethann Wetzel. We've been through a lot together, and I'm sure there were times when my sanity was in serious doubt. To Paula Turner for her love and support. To Liza Shuttleworth and her dog Louie for taste testing so many recipes.

My thanks to all of you who have given me your help, love, and support:

Ben, Liz, Nick, & Natasha Stanton
Carol Ann Blinken
David & Sally Blinken
Jon Blinken
Linda Tishman
Ruth & Howard W. Koch
Eliane, Mark & Rachel Fahim
Catherine Venturini
Heidi Frieder
Adrian Leeds

Special thanks goes to Lewis Turner. His participation in Lip Smackers has bred new life to my dreams and goals. I tell him to always keep the magic coming.

CONTENTS

PREFACE

One of the first things I wanted to have after graduating college was a dog; not just an ordinary dog, but a Chinese Shar-pei, as this breed had always fascinated me. After a great deal of searching I found the perfect one - Webster. When I got him home, he looked like one big ball of wrinkles and except for his head he has since grown into them.

When Webster was just a few months old, I began noticing digestive and skin problems. Our veterinarian took tests and diagnosed him as being allergic to soy. At the time, I thought it would be easy enough to find a food that would agree with him and meet my high standards for nutritional value. I discovered a kibble that he enjoyed, but I ran into some problems finding biscuits for treats.

Most of the biscuits were made up of ingredients that either I didn't want Webster to eat or he simply didn't like. The quest had begun to find the right biscuit. After many trials and tribulations, I decided to test my talents in the kitchen and create a biscuit myself. In this way, I'd have control of the ingredients and besides......how difficult could it be to bake a dog biscuit? I was surprised to find that it was very complicated. I went through batch after batch after batch. Either they didn't work or Webster would turn up his bulbous nose and politely walk away.

It took almost a year before finding the right combination of ingredients. I noticed that one particular batch I had removed from the oven had a mouth watering aroma. Before the biscuits had hardened, I tasted them and found these were particularly good. After they had cooled, I called Webster over for the ultimate test. Not only did he eat one, he wanted another. I felt that this recipe had definite possibilities.

Before long, people dropped in to find out what the delicious smell was. They, in turn, participated in the "taste test". The general response was that the biscuits were a bit bland, but not bad. When I divulged that these were made for Webster, some laughed and others had "interesting" expressions.

During the holiday season I became inundated with requests from friends and family to make up orders. As demand increased, I gave more and more thought to

enhancing what was, by then, a part-time job.

I finally decided to put all of my efforts into producing and merchandising "Webster's Cookies". My husband, Tim, and I were discussing the cookie when he turned to me and said, "we'll call them Lip Smackers".

Originally we packed the cookies in Chinese to go cartons with a drawing of Webster on the front. Many hours were spent baking biscuits, labelling cartons, hand packing and delivering them to stores. This was only the beginning.

The carton soon changed to a bag, and the number of stores carrying Lip Smackers grew. With this increased popularity, we have created a new eye-catching box design.

Since cooking for both the two and four legged members of my family was one of my greatest pleasures, I kept an extensive file of my favorite recipes. One day it struck me that there were others who would enjoy a cookbook on canine cuisine. I began the process of writing, re-writing, cooking, tasting and testing. Once again, I found myself involved in a project that was much more exciting than ever imagined. I have created easy-to-prepare recipes that will be fun for the whole family. This will be the first in a series of cookbooks. ENJOY!

Wendy Boyd-Smith

-Wendy Boyd-Smith

INTRODUCTION

The purpose of this book is to provide suggestions on how to "liven" up your dog's diet.   I have prepared all the recipes in this book and fed them to Webster and other dogs who seemed to genuinely enjoy them. These recipes are simply a supplement to your dog's diet and are not designed to replace it.

If you question any of the recipe ingredients or preparations please seek the advice of your veterinarian. After all, each dog's needs and reactions are different. I experienced this with Webster and it was his colitis condition that led to the creation of Lip Smackers' dog biscuits.

One of the objectives in writing this book was to encourage parents to bring their children into the kitchen. Using their dog as the incentive might act as a springboard for other activities like helping out with the family dinner.

Interestingly enough I have had especially good response from parents with handicapped children. Due to the ease of preparation of most of the recipes, those with physical and/or mental handicaps can take part in some way. Activities like these help to build confidence while learning skills in the process. They then receive the extra bonus of having helped make something for their pet.

You'll find a number of recipes titled, "From Kelly Ann's Kitchen." My dear friend Kelly Ann McNabb has certainly taught me a lot about cooking. It gives me great pleasure to include each of the recipes she provided. This is the first of many projects we will work on together. Thank you Kelly.

Eliane Fahim, Paula Turner and Bethann Wetzel who contributed delicious recipes for your enjoyment. As you can see, all my friends have lent their support to this book.

Although our awareness in the area of human nutrition has improved dramatically, there has not been much of an impact on our pet's foods. We hope to help you become aware of their nutritional needs by talking with your veterinarian and reading

about what you are feeding your pet. Preservatives and salt do the same things to pets as they do to humans.

Perhaps the best thing to do now is to turn to the section that intrigues you, get the kids (both two and four legged) and start cooking.

SEND US YOUR RECIPES.

Please write us and include all your healthy-ingredient recipes and suggestions. If there is a lip-smacking response to them in our taste test, we will include them in our next book (with your permission.)

A WORD FROM WEBSTER AND MAX

Hi, my name is Webster and I'd like to share my story with all of you:

My first memories of Wendy are from my pup days in Atlanta, GA. I was literally one mass of wrinkles and got lots of rather strange looks; but Wendy kept telling me people stared because I was special. We appeared in many dog shows but I was always so nervous that I would usually end up with an upset stomach. It wasn't long before we found out I had a problem called colitis.

Wendy began experimenting with all sorts of foods to see how my stomach would react. I remember pots and pans flying around the kitchen and a lot of cooking going on! It was cookie heaven. Some tasted good, some were fair and to be honest, some were so bad that I had to escape outside. But I'll never forget this one particular afternoon when she removed from her oven the best smelling biscuits ever. Wendy named them "Webster's Cookies", but now they're called Lip Smackers: Different name but still my recipe!!

It was during this time that Max came into our lives when he moved next door, and soon, we became the best of friends. (Max's Mom is pretty cool too — She gives a mean water bowl!) When Wendy decided to put Max's picture along with Eleanor — the pretty Dalmation — on our spiffy new Lip Smackers' box, I was one happy camper! Max is much more outgoing than me, and thrives on attention. His ultimate fantasy is to be on the cover of "Dog World". I much prefer the quiet life.

Now I want to fill you in on this exciting cookbook you're about to experience.

For years, we were "hounding" Wendy to print up some of her favorite recipes. It seemed like there were always friends and relatives visiting us, and Wendy would constantly be whipping up a creation or two. Occasionally, she had help: Aunt Beth would cook up a pretty terrific rice dish along with some very outrageous desserts, and Kelly spoiled us with a lot of her delicious dishes. Max and I insisted their recipes be a part of this book so you could enjoy them too.

Barney, with pencil and pad constantly in hand, has totally kept us in awe with his clever and humourus ways of sketching. I wonder if Wendy showed him our family album!

Before I bow out let me give Lewis one of my huge, sloppy kisses for helping us write our tale.

Now... I promised Max he could share a few words with you. Beleive me, that's no easy task 'cause he can talk forever. Ok Max, it's your turn:

Well, finally I get to tell you my side of the story. Oh, oh... Sniff, Sniff, Sniff... Smells like lunch is being served. Sorry, can't talk now... Gotta run. *Enjoy the book...*

Webster & Max

16

BEFORE YOU BEGIN

A lot of recipes throughout this book call for boiled chicken livers or boiled chicken pieces. To do this, in a large sauce pan or small stock pot full of cold water (approximately 5 cups of cold water to every pound of meat) add 1 or 2 onions and a bay leaf for flavor. (The onions can later be ground up with the chicken livers, but always remove the bay leaf.) Bring chicken pieces or the livers to a boil and simmer for 25-30 minutes uncovered. Drain. They can be served plain or used in other recipes. ALWAYS wait for food to cool before serving.

I have specifically selected ingredients that are fresh, wholesome, and readily available. Also, adding fresh chopped parsley not only tastes great but has natural chlorophyll which helps freshen breath. You can purchase brewers yeast at a health food store. Feel free to add this to any recipe (as in the cookie recipes) since it claims to help control fleas and aids in digestion. Most of my recipes call for beef or chicken stock (or broth). I like the low salt version which can be purchased in a can from the supermarket. If you wish to make your own stock, the recipe can be found in chapter 13.

Snicks and Snacks from

Webster and Max

THE SUPER BOWL PARTY

In January **The Boys** become obsessed with football, or at least from my point of view its an OBSESSION. As the play-offs draw to a close and the Superbowl is upon us, bets are placed and verbal invites ring out — SUPERBOWL PARTY AT WENDY'S PLACE.

Making snacks for your pet doesn't have to be long and involved. This section is simplicity at its best, a key to a last minute doggie delight.

Fix these sporty specialities when you want to score **BIG TIME!**

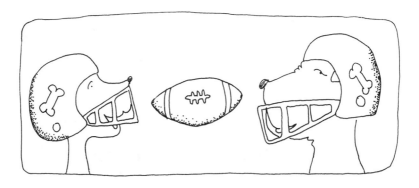

CHEESE TOAST POINTS
(serves 6)

6 slices brown cocktail bread cut in triangles
3 tablespoons grated Parmesan
1 teaspoon paprika

Sprinkle cheese and paprika on bread. Toast under broiler until lightly brown.

MEATBALL COCKTAIL
(serves 6)

1 pound ground beef
1/2 cup cooked brown rice
1 small onion chopped
1 tablespoon ketchup
1 egg beaten
2 tablespoons fresh chopped parsley

Preheat oven to 350 degrees.

Mix all ingredients together. Form meat into small balls. Bake in a 9 x 12 baking dish for 45 - 55 minutes. Cool and serve.

QUICHE LORRAINE FOR THE BACON AND EGG LOVER
(without the pastry pie shell)
(serves 6)

6 slices low salt bacon cut in half
12 thin slices Swiss cheese cut in strips
4 eggs
1 tablespoon all purpose flour
2 cups light cream
1 1/2 tablespoons melted butter
pinch of nutmeg

Preheat oven to 375 degrees.

Cook bacon and set aside. Beat eggs and add flour, nutmeg and cream. Stir in melted butter. Place bacon and cheese in layers in a Pyrex or glass pie pan. Pour egg mixture over and bake for 45 minutes to 1 hour. Serve cool.

LIVER DROPS
(serves 6)

1 pound chicken livers
5 cups water
1 chicken bouillon cube
1 small onion (chopped)
1 cup seasoned bread crumbs mixed with two tablespoons wheat germ

Combine water and bouillon cube into a large saucepan and bring to a boil. Add onion and liver and boil until tender. Drain. Take liver and onion and place in blender or food processor. Blend until mixture is stiff with small chunks, and form into small balls. Roll meatballs in bread crumb mixture. Place on a lightly greased cookie sheet and bake until golden brown. Let liver drops cool and serve. This may be frozen in single serving portions.

GREAT TREAT FOR ENTICING A DOG AT ALL THOSE DOG SHOWS, OR JUST A LITTLE TONGUE PLEASER!

PROSCIUTTO WITH CHEESE STICKS
(serves 6)

6 slices of boiled ham
1/2 block cheddar cheese

> **Prosciutto is far too expensive, but it sounds good. We use boiled ham and Webster and Maxwell love it. But they still like to call it Prosciutto.**

Slice cheese into sticks and place one in center of each slice of ham. Roll. Serve immediately.

EGGS FOR THE DEVIL ON A DIET
(serves 6)

1 1/4 cups nonfat cottage cheese
6 hard boiled eggs, halved. Set aside the yolks
1/2 teaspoon onion powder
1/2 teaspoon garlic powder

In a blender or food processor, mix egg yolks, cottage cheese, onion, garlic and blend well. Pipe (spoon) into the egg halves.

You may garnish egg halves with a sprinkle of paprika.

TUNA PATE
When Plain Tuna Fish Just Won't Do
(serves 4)

Many are surprised to find that their pooch likes fish and that cats have not cornered the market.

>1-12 ounce can of tuna
>1 tablespoon olive oil
>2 teaspoons grated onion
>1 teaspoon lemon juice
>4 tablespoons cottage cheese

Blend all ingredients in a blender or food processor. Add lemon juice. Mold and chill until ready to serve.

Dark tuna is preferred in our house as it is richer and more flavorful. But what's most important..... Webster and Max love it!

Puppy Love

ST. VALENTINE'S DAY

How many winter hours have we all spent staring into a fire, and into our loved one's eyes, eating foods to warm our hearts.

Stews are always healthy as they contain various food groups. Max especially enjoys the carrots. I don't think this vegetable has improved his eyesight, although he never has a problem finding his plate.

FROM ELIANE'S KITCHEN:

RICE FOR THE TRUE RICE LOVER!
(serves 4)

l cup long grain white rice
l small bunch of vermicelli(thin spaghetti)
l 1/2 cups water
l tablespoon butter

Break vermicelli into small pieces and saute with butter in a sauce pan until slightly brown. Add rice, brown slightly then add water. Bring to a boil, cover and simmer for 20 minutes. Serve at room temperature.

Webster's favorite!! He likes to add a dollop of plain yogurt!!

A STEW TO WARM ANY HEART
Beef Stew
(serves 6)

1 pound stewing beef, cubed
20 small button onions, peeled
5 carrots, chunked
2 1/2 cups boiling water mixed with 2 beef bouillon cubes
1 cup canned corn
1 bay leaf
2 cloves chopped garlic
1 tablespoon yellow corn flour mixed with 2 tablespoons cold water

Preheat oven to 325 degrees.

Mix the first seven ingredients. Bake in a Dutch oven for 2 hours. Add corn flour mixture and mix well. Return to oven for another 30 minutes.

For the dog on a low salt diet, you may substitute beef bouillon cubes for low salt beef broth: One cup water with 1 1/2 cups beef broth.

This can be frozen in single serving portions.

> **Always remember to remove the bay leaf before serving.**

CHICKEN STEW

(serves 6)

1 pound deboned chicken, cubed (light or dark meat)
10 small button onions, peeled
5 carrots, chunked
1 cup peas (frozen can be used)
2 1/2 cups boiling water mixed with 2 chicken bouillon cubes
1 bay leaf
1 tablespoon yellow corn flour mixed with 2 tablespoons cold water

Preheat oven to 325 degrees.

Mix first six ingredients. Bake in a Dutch oven for 1 hour. Add corn flour mixture and mix well. Return to oven for another 30 minutes.

For the dog on low salt diets, you may substitute beef bouillon cubes for low salt chicken broth: 1 cup water with 1 1/2 cups low salt chicken broth.

This can be frozen in single serving portions.

May serve at room temperature over Kibble.

Always remember to remove the bay leaf before serving.

BASIC BURGER FOR TWO
(serves 2)

1 pound ground beef
1 tablespoon onion powder
1 tablespoon fresh chopped parsley
2 tablespoons A-1 Sauce ®

In a large bowl, mix all ingredients together. Form meat mixture into two hamburger patties and grill until done.

> **No frills, but basics can
> be fun as well as healthy.**

Green And Lean

ST. PATTY'S DAY

On St. Patrick's day I woke to find a world gone green and perhaps a bit mad. Before me there lay a breakfast of Irish delight. Green ...green.....green eggs, green milk, green oatmeal. The key here is green. If Dr. Seuss could do it, then why not Maureen McNulty Wetzel?

We loved it so, that to this day we still celebrate St Patty's day in a very green way.

MAUREEN'S GREEN EGGS
(serves 2)

2 eggs
2 drops green food coloring (adjust to desired color)
1/4 cup cooked diced ham
1 teaspoon butter or margarine

Beat eggs, add green food coloring and ham. Heat skillet with butter or margarine. Pour in egg mixture and cook slowly over medium heat until done.

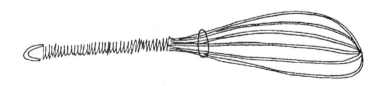

FROM KELLY ANN'S KITCHEN

HALF BAKED BROCCOLI
(serves 4)

1 large bunch of broccoli (cut into bite size pieces)
1/2 cup extra light olive oil
1/2 cup fresh bread crumbs
1 cup wheat germ
1/2 cup Swiss cheese, grated
2 hard boiled eggs
2 cloves crushed fresh garlic

Preheat oven to 325 degrees.

Steam broccoli for 5 - 7 minutes. Saute bread crumbs, garlic and wheat germ until tender and golden brown (3 - 4 minutes). Alternately layer casserole dish with broccoli and bread crumb mixture. Repeat until both mixtures are used up. Top casserole with sliced hard boiled eggs and Swiss cheese. Bake for 25 minutes.

FROM KELLY ANN'S KITCHEN

GREEN AND MEAN ZUCCHINI CASSEROLE
(serves 6)

4 cups grated zucchini (set in a colander with 1/2 tablespoon
    salt over it to drain)
1/2 cup grated Swiss cheese
1 cup all purpose flour
2 teaspoons fast acting baking powder
2 eggs, beaten
1 cup half and half
salt and pepper to taste

Preheat oven to 325 degrees.

Mix all ingredients together and put into buttered baking dish. Bake for 35-45 minutes until golden brown.

A Sunday Munch

EASTER BRUNCH

Ask any pup what they do on Easter. Most will say, "Hunt for the Easter eggs!" Max and Webster always run through my garden (oh dear!) in clear competition of who will collect the most eggs. When all is said and done, baskets are full, the feast enjoyed and the soil has been turned for spring flowers.

HEALTH JACKS
Pancakes For The Easter Brunch
(serves 4)

3/4 cup rolled oats
3/4 cup lowfat milk
1/2 teaspoon baking soda
1/4 cup whole wheat flour
1 egg beaten
1/2 teaspoon vanilla

In a blender or food processor chop oats. In a large bowl, mix oats and milk. Put aside for five minutes. Add baking soda, flour, egg, vanilla and mix. Spoon small amounts into a hot buttered skillet. Serve with a dollop of cottage cheese.

These flap jacks don't weigh you down.
I've made them for the family (two and four legged).
Be careful with syrup of any kind — most tend to be fatty.

FROM KELLY ANN'S KITCHEN

SO WHY DO THEY CALL THEM SCOTCH EGGS?

(serves 6)

3 tablespoons olive oil
2 pounds ground beef (may substitute half the ground beef with
    ground pork)
1/2 cup bread crumbs
1 tablespoon fresh parsley
2 tablespoons fresh Parmesan cheese (finely grated)
2 eggs beaten lightly
6 hard boiled eggs

Preheat oven to 325 degrees.

Mix ground beef, parsley, cheese, bread crumbs and 2 eggs until blended.
Mold ground beef mixture around shelled hard boiled eggs.
Brown in olive oil, then transfer to baking dish.
Bake for 20-25 minutes or until done.

NUTHIN' BUT MUTTON (AND VEGGIE) STEW
(serves 6)

2 tablespoons olive oil
1 1/2 pounds cubed lamb shoulder
1 large onion, chopped
2 cloves of garlic, minced
1/2 cup tomato sauce (low salt)
2 cups water
1/2 cup carrots, chopped
1/2 cup peas (frozen can be used)
1/2 cup zucchini, cubed

Heat oil and brown meat. Reduce heat, add onions and garlic and cook until brown. Add tomatoes, carrots, zucchini and water. Simmer 1 1/2 hours. Add peas and simmer another 30 minutes.

This can be frozen in single serving portions.

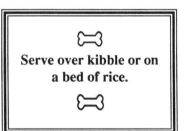

Serve over kibble or on
a bed of rice.

A LOAF WITH SOME REAL SPRING
VEGETABLE LOAF
(serves 6)

6 cups cooked brown rice
1 clove garlic, chopped
1 medium yellow onion, chopped
1 large tomato, chopped
1 teaspoon oregano
1/4 cup fresh parsley, chopped
2 eggs — beaten
1 cup grated carrots
1/2 cup grated zucchini
1 cup low salt chicken broth
1 tablespoon olive oil

Preheat oven to 350 degrees. In a fry pan heat oil. Saute garlic, onion and tomato for 5 minutes. Combine all ingredients in a large bowl and mix well. In a lightly greased loaf pan spoon in mixture. Bake for 50 minutes, cool and serve.

May Day....
May Day....

Spring is upon us and the celebration of May Day is typified by a light fare served on linen clothed tables beneath the shade of an old oak tree. As the meal is laid out Webster's curiosities draw him about the garden where the colorful blooms of newly born flowers lend their fragrance to our picnic.....Now if we could only get Max to land the aircraft, we could begin our meal.

TUNA DELIGHT
WITH A BROCCOLI BITE
(serves 4)

1 1/2 cups cooked elbow macaroni
1 cup low fat milk
1 cup grated cheddar cheese
1 cup chopped fresh broccoli
1 can tuna — drained
1 tablespoon chopped onion
1/4 cup seasoned bread crumbs mixed with 2 tablespoons wheat germ

Preheat oven to 350 degrees.

Combine all ingredients except bread crumb mixture and mix well. Spoon into a lightly greased casserole dish. Sprinkle with bread crumb mixture. Bake for 30 minutes. Cool and serve.

SPINACH RICE

(serves 6)

1 package frozen chopped spinach
1/2 cup onion, chopped
1 clove garlic, chopped
1/2 cup carrots, chopped
1/2 teaspoon thyme leaves
2 cups cooked brown rice
1 cup non-fat cottage cheese
1 tablespoon olive oil

Preheat oven to 350 degrees.

Defrost spinach. Saute garlic and onions in oil until soft (approximately 5 minutes.) Mix all ingredients together and spoon into a lightly greased baking dish. Bake for 25-30 minutes.

TURKEY CUTLETS
(serves 4)

4 boneless turkey breast, skinned and pounded very thin
1 1/2 cups seasoned bread crumbs mixed with 2 tablespoons
     wheat germ
2 eggs, beaten
4 tablespoons olive oil

Dip turkey in egg mixture. Roll in bread crumbs. Heat oil and saute turkey until brown on both sides and cooked through. Slice in strips and serve.

The Wedding

For a truly special occasion, a little creativity can go a long way. The wedding is always a special event. When the day finally arrives to take those special vows, a feast will be in order!

THE MAIN EVENT — BRISKET FOR 20?
Did You Say Brisket Dinner?

1 small brisket of beef
2 onions, thinly sliced
1 cup low salt tomato sauce
3 tablespoons vegetable oil
1 tablespoon salt and pepper, mixed together
2 cups low salt beef broth

In a Dutch oven, heat oil. Season meat with salt and pepper and sear on both sides. Lower heat, add onions, tomato sauce and beef broth. Cover tightly and simmer for about 2 1/2 - 3 hours until the meat is tender. Cool and serve. This can be stored in single serving size containers and frozen.

For those truly special occasions,
A little creativity can go a long way.
This is another dish that can be put
Away for another day.

A BROWN RICE FIT TO BE FED

(serves 4

1 cup instant brown rice
1 large onion, chopped
1 tablespoon chopped garlic
2 cups low salt beef broth

In a medium sauce pan, bring beef broth to a boil. Add remaining ingredients. Cover and simmer for 20 minutes. Recipe may be doubled.

**Brown rice is
wonderful mixed in
with kibble.**

COOKIES — MAX'S MID-MEAL MUNCH

(4-5 dozen)

2 cups whole wheat flour
2/3 cups yellow corn meal
1/2 cup shelled sunflower seeds
2 eggs mixed with 1/4 cup lowfat milk
2 tablespoons corn oil
1/2 cup low salt beef broth

GLAZE
Beat 1 egg . Lightly brush on cookie before baking.

Preheat oven to 350 degrees.

In a large bowl, mix dry ingredients and seeds together. Add oil, broth and egg mixture. Your dough should be firm. Let sit 15-20 minutes. On a lightly floured surface, roll out dough 1/4 inch thick. Cut into shapes and brush with glaze. Bake for 25-35 minutes until golden brown. Take out and cool. Store cookies in an airtight container.

This dough can also used for The Wedding Cake.

> **In-between meal snacks are okay
> if made the healthy way.**

TRIPLE DECKER DELIGHT

A Jewel Of A Wedding Cake
(serves 2: One for the Bride and one for the Groom!)

The Wedding Cake is a three-step process. If you are going to bake and assemble the cake the same day, allow approximately three hours. If you don't want to prepare it all at once; you can make the cookies, liver filling and frosting a day or two ahead. Keep the cookies in an air-tight container, and refrigerate the liver filling and frosting.

BASE OF THE CAKE

Use Max's Mid-Meal Munch cookie recipe. Roll out the dough and cut six 3-inch round circles, 1/4 inch thick. Bake at 350 degrees for 25-35 minutes until golden brown.

LIVER FILLING

1/2 pound liver
2 tablespoons butter
1 small onion, chopped
1 hard boiled egg

Melt butter in a medium fry pan. Saute liver and onions over medium heat for 10-15 minutes. Drain and cool. Chop liver and onion mixture in a food processor or blender until a thick paste is formed.

Chop the egg and set aside.

(continued)

Triple Decker Delight *(continued)*

FROSTING

1 cup non-fat cottage cheese

In a blender or food processor, mix until smooth.

Spread a medium layer of the liver mixture on top of a cookie. Lightly sprinkle chopped egg. Place another cookie on top and repeat process. Place the third and final cookie on top and frost the cake with the cottage cheese frosting. Serve the cake whole

Specialties With Sparkle

INDEPENDENCE DAY PICNIC

Lay out a blanket, put up an umbrella and pull out a frisbee. For our family, Fourth of July has always been a day to party, swim, and eat to the point of contentment. When all are fully satiated pick your spot on the blanket and enjoy an evening sky full of specialties and sparkles.

STAR SPANGLED MEAT LOAF
(serves 4)

1 pound ground beef
2 tablespoons rolled oats
1/2 cup cooked brown rice
3 tablespoons chopped onion
3 tablespoons chopped garlic
2 tablespoons fresh chopped parsley
1 tablespoon ketchup
1 egg beaten
1 teaspoon Worchestershire®
3 hard boiled eggs

Preheat oven to 350 degrees.

Mix all ingredients well. Place mixture in a loaf pan. Make a small valley in the loaf, and place the hard boiled eggs in the center. Cover the eggs with the meat. (DON'T FORGET TO TAKE THE SHELLS OFF THE EGGS.) Bake for 1 hour or until cooked through.

FROM KELLY ANN'S KITCHEN:

YOUR POOCH WILL LOVE THESE "PASTA-BILITIES"

(serves 4)

4-6 pounds spaghetti squash
1/4 cup olive oil
2 cloves fresh garlic (minced or pressed)
2-3 plum tomatoes chopped and seeded
1/4 cup fresh cilantro picked off stem (optional)
1 medium zucchini chopped
1/2 pound fresh mushrooms sliced

Preheat oven to 400 degrees.

Cut squash lengthwise (discard seeds) and place cut side down in a baking dish 1/4 full of water. Bake for 45 minutes until tender. Let cool.

> **Kelly really surprised me with this one. Webster and Max spent all of 30 seconds looking and sniffing before digging in.**

Heat 1/2 olive oil with garlic in saute pan. Saute tomatoes and zucchini 3-4 minutes on medium high heat. Add mushrooms and cook 1 minute. Optional: Finish with chopped cilantro.

Using a fork, scrape out the center of the squash — the strands will look just like spaghetti — and saute for 1 minute in remaining olive oil. Top with sauce and serve.

PUPSICLES FOR A HOT DAY

This recipe is quick, easy and fun. Probably best to serve outside to avoid water on your carpet.

> 2 cups low salt beef or chicken broth
> 2 -3 ice cube trays
> 2/3 cup water

Mix 2/3 cup water with 2 cups of beef or chicken broth. Pour into ice trays. Place in freezer and serve cold. For an extra treat, add a rawhide stick halfway through the freezing. Serve outside.

Generally, dogs love to chew on ice cubes. Natural food colorings can be added. Ice cubes are especially helpful during summer months, as they keep the drinking water cool and the pup hydrated. While travelling, ice cubes will replace water in your pet carrier's water dish. This will help to prevent spillage.

For Puppy Owners: Rubbing ice cubes on your pup's gums can help relieve those pains associated with new teeth and often diminish teething tendencies. Wrapping the ice cubes in an old clean rag provides your little one with a helpful fun toy.

The Birthday Bonanza

MAX'S FAVORITES

I'M THE BIRTHDAY BOY. ITS MY BIRTHDAY WEEK. I'M HAVING A BIG PARTY WITH LOTS OF PRESENTS AND CAKE because... I'M THE BIRTHDAY BOY AND YOU HAVE TO BE NICE TO ME.

SLOPPY JOE DINNER
A Meal Meant To Be Messy
(serves 4)

1 pound ground beef
1/2 cup chopped onion
1 tablespoon chopped garlic
1/2 cup chopped carrots
1 cup low salt beef broth

Mix all ingredients together and place in a fry pan. Cook over medium heat until meat is cooked through. Drain most of the fat and add the beef broth. Simmer for 10 minutes. If you desire more gravy, add more beef broth.

FROM KELLY ANN'S KITCHEN:

CHILLY CHICKEN RICE SUPREME
A Salad For All Seasons!
(serves 4)

1 1/2 cups cold cooked brown rice
1/2 cup diced cooked chicken
1/2 cup diced cooked carrots
1/4 cup chopped scallions
1/4 cup chopped parsley
1 tablespoon olive oil

In a large bowl, mix all ingredients and toss with the olive oil. This is perfect for that birthday picnic!

> On those hot summer days when appetites are at a low, this dish perks them up. Chicken rice is a favorite dish of Webster's. He always comes back for more.

BETHANN'S CARROT RICE

(serves 6)

2 cups cooked brown rice
2 cups grated carrots
1 cup cooked chunked chicken
1 cup grated Swiss cheese
1 large yellow onion, chopped
1 egg, beaten
  1/4 cup low salt chicken broth
1/4 cup vegetable oil
1/4 cup chopped parsley

Preheat oven to 350 degrees.

Mix rice with all ingredients. Spoon into lightly greased casserole dish and bake for 50 minutes to 1 hour. Cool and serve.

COOKIES WITH CHICKEN BROTH
Max's Midnight Snack
(48-60 cookies)

2 cups whole wheat flour
2/3 cups yellow corn meal
1/2 cup shelled sunflower seeds
2 eggs mixed with 1/4 cup lowfat milk
2 tablespoons corn oil
1/2 cup chicken broth

GLAZE
Beat 1 egg. Lightly brush on cookie before baking.

Preheat oven to 350 degrees.

In a large bowl, mix dry ingredients and seeds together. Add oil, broth and egg mixture. Your dough should be firm. Let sit 15-20 minutes. On a lightly floured surface, roll out dough 1/4 inch thick. Cut into shapes and brush with glaze. Bake for 25-35 minutes until golden brown. Take out and cool. Store cookies in an airtight container.

The Hunt Lunch
(WITHOUT THE FOX)

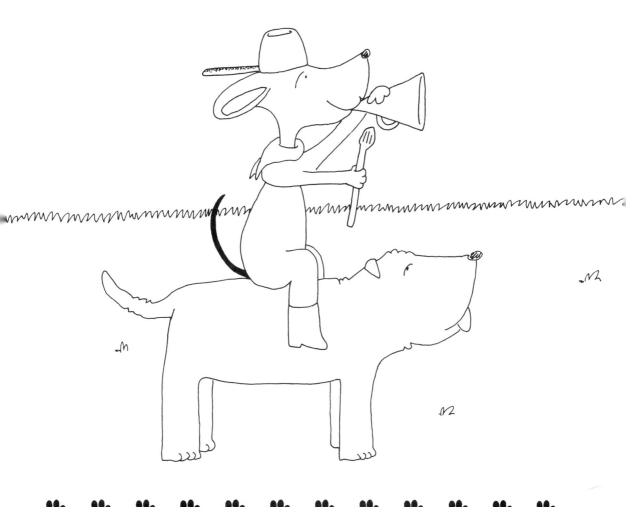

September breeds a nip in the air and a collage of breeze filled fall foliage.

Although the boys have never been on a hunt, you can bet your right paw they would never miss the Hunt Lunch or an opportunity to spend a day at the stables.

CHICKEN KABOBS
(serves 6)

1/2 cup vegetable oil
1/4 cup low salt soy sauce
1/4 teaspoon garlic powder
1/4 teaspoon onion
1/4 cup orange juice
4 chicken breasts cut into 2 inch pieces
1 medium onion quartered
2 large zucchini

Combine first 5 ingredients with the chicken pieces and marinate for 2 hours in refrigerator. Remove chicken from marinade and alternately place chicken, onion and zucchini on skewers. Brush with leftover marinade. Place on grill and cook for 20 minutes. Remove from skewers. Cool and serve.

EGG DROP SOUP
(serves 6)

4 cups low salt chicken broth
1/2 cup chopped carrots
1/2 cup chopped celery
2 eggs beaten
1 tablespoon low salt soy sauce

    Bring the chicken broth to a boil. Add chopped carrots, celery and soy sauce. Simmer for 15-20 minutes. Bring soup back to a boil and slowly add beaten eggs with one hand while the other hand is stirring the soup. Let egg cook for 5 minutes. The egg will look like string. Cool and serve with kibble as <u>croutons.</u>

PAULA T.'S RICE
(serves 4)

1 cup long grain white rice
1/2 cup chopped onion
1/2 cup chopped parsley
2 cups low salt chicken broth
1 tablespoon butter or margarine

> **Can be served with Egg Drop Soup.**

    In a sauce pan, melt butter or margarine and saute onion until soft. Add rice and mix. Add chicken broth and parsley. Bring to a boil. Cover and simmer for 20 minutes. Remove from heat and let sit covered for an additional 5 minutes. Cool and serve.

PEANUT-OAT COOKIES

Directly From The Peanut Gallery —
Guaranteed Not To Stick To The
Roof Of Your Mouth!
(24 cookies)

1/2 cup butter or margarine, softened
1/2 cup brown sugar
1 egg, beaten
1/4 cup peanut butter (plain)
1 cup whole wheat flour
1/2 teaspoon baking soda
1 cup rolled oats
2 tablespoons wheat germ

Preheat oven to 350 degrees.

Cream together butter and sugar. Add egg and beat well. Stir in peanut butter until smooth. Mix flour and baking soda; then add to mixture. Mix in oats until well blended. Drop by spoonful onto greased cookie sheet and flatten with a fork to make a design .Bake for 12-14 minutes.

> **These cookies are rich and should be given one or two at a time**
> **on very special occasions; like Christmas or New Years.**
> **Webster and Max love them!**

Ghosts, Goblins And Doggie Delights

HALLOWEEN NIGHT

Trick or Treat ...Trick or Treat...The Boys like to see how many sweets they can eat. I have created the costume party as a healthy alternative to trick or treating. Max is the first in his costume and the last to leave the table when I serve my Halloween fare.

FROM KELLY ANN'S KITCHEN:

OPEN SESAME CHICKEN
(serves 4)

4 boneless chicken breasts, skinned and pounded 1/4 inch thick
1 cup toasted sesame seeds
2 tablespoons olive oil
1 teaspoon thyme*
1 teaspoon sweet basil *
1 teaspoon rosemary *
1/2 teaspoon salt
1/2 teaspoon black pepper
2 eggs lightly beaten
1/3 cup all purpose flour
* dried herbs preferred

> **When cool, slice and serve on a bed of kibble.**

Preheat oven to 350 degrees.

In the first bowl, combine sesame seeds and herbs. In a second bowl, beat eggs. In a third bowl, mix flour, pepper and salt. Dredge chicken breasts into flour, then into eggs, and press into sesame seeds. Brown in olive oil . Bake for 25 minutes.

FROM KELLY ANN'S KITCHEN:

LOW-CAL GRILLED VEGETABLES FOR THE BARBECUE
(serves 4)

1 large red pepper (halved and seeded)
1 large yellow pepper (halved and seeded)
2 zucchinis, halved lengthwise
2 yellow squash, halved lengthwise
6 large scallions, both ends trimmed
1 large eggplant, cut into 1 inch thick rounds
3 purple onions, peeled and cut in half

Baste all veggies with olive oil on both sides (I use a pastry brush). Start with the onions, cook 2 minutes and then add eggplant, zucchini and squash. Let grill 3 - 4 minutes, occasionally basting with the olive oil. As vegetables are done cooking, set aside in a bowl. This allows natural juices to surface. When all vegetables are cooked, cut into bite-sized pieces.

> I think you will be surprised at just how much dogs enjoy vegetables when given the chance and the right preparation. Most would no sooner chomp on a head of lettuce than you or I, but with a little creativity thrown in, you just might scare yourself!

FRIED RICE
(serves 6)

2 cups cold cooked brown rice
1/2 cup cooked peas
1/2 cup chunked ham
1/2 cup cooked chunked carrots
3 tablespoons vegetable oil
1 tablespoon low salt soy sauce
1/2 cup onion, chopped

In a large skillet, heat oil. Add onion and carrots. Saute until onions are translucent. Add peas, ham, rice and soy sauce. Cook for 10 minutes over medium heat while stirring.

BLACK AND WHITE MUFFINS (CAROB CHIP)
(12 small muffins)

1/4 cup brown sugar
1/4 cup light molasses
1/2 cup corn oil
1 cup lowfat milk
1 teaspoon vanilla
2 cups all-purpose flour
1 tablespoon baking powder
1/2 teaspoon baking soda
1/2 cup carob chips (available at health food store)

Preheat oven to 400 degrees.

In a large bowl, add brown sugar, molasses, corn oil, milk and vanilla. Mix well. Then add all the dry ingredients. Mix well. Slowly fold in the carob chips. Spoon mixture into muffin tins. Bake for 20 minutes. Cool. Can be frozen in single servings.

> **Remember to always use carob instead of chocolate.
> Chocolate can be very dangerous to your pet!**

Let's Talk Turkey

THANKSGIVING FEAST

In our house, Thanksgiving is the biggest party of the year. The Manhattan Turkey has become a tradition for man, woman and dog alike. When we all sit down to Thanksgiving dinner, and the house is bursting with hungry guests, no one feels left out of the festivities.

BIRD IN A PAN
Turkey Loaf with Stuffing
(serves 2)

1 pound ground turkey
1 cup cooked brown rice
1 egg, beaten
1 cup low salt chicken broth
1 cup of your favorite stuffing
1/2 cup chopped celery
1/2 cup chopped carrots
1/2 cup chopped parsley
1 1/2 tablespoons chopped garlic
3 tablespoons chopped onion

Preheat oven to 350 degrees.

In a large bowl, mix turkey, egg, rice, celery, carrots, parsley, garlic and onion. Blend well. In a medium bowl, blend chicken broth and stuffing. Add to turkey mixture. Shape into loaf pan, and bake for 1-1/2 hours or until done.

> **This has no bones and generally no leftovers.**

CHICKEN LOAF
More Cluck for your Buck
(serves 2)

1 pound ground chicken
1 cup cooked brown rice
1 egg beaten
1/4 cup fresh chopped parsley
2 tablespoons fresh minced garlic
3 tablespoons wheat germ
1/2 cup chopped carrots

> If the Colonel ever opens a restaurant serving canine fare, chicken loaf would become the most begged for entree.

Preheat oven to 350 degrees.

In a large bowl, mix all ingredients. Form into a loaf pan, and bake for 1 hour or until done. Cool and serve. Slice Chicken Loaf and serve over kibble.

ZUCCHINI PANCAKES
(serves 4)

3 cups coarsely grated and peeled zucchini
1 egg
1/2 cup flour
1 teaspoon baking powder

(continued)

Zucchini Pancakes (continued)

In a large bowl, combine zucchini and egg. Add flour and baking powder. Mix well. Drop by the spoonful on a hot skillet with a little oil or butter. Cook until light brown on both sides.

FROM KELLY ANN'S KITCHEN:

MUSHROOM AND CHEESE RICE
(serves 6)

2 tablespoons unsalted butter
3 cups cooked rice (preferably brown)
1 6-oz package cream cheese
2 eggs
1 1/2 pounds sliced fresh mushrooms
1 can (10 oz) evaporated milk
4 scallions (both ends cut off)
1 cup shredded Jarlsberg cheese

Preheat oven to 350 degrees.

Blend cream cheese, eggs, evaporated milk and cheese. Saute mushrooms and scallions until brown and drain off juices. Mix rice, mushrooms and cheese mixture together. Put in buttered baking dish, and bake for 1 hour covered. Serve with plenty of fresh water.

The Yuletide Dog

CHRISTMAS DINNER

Dashing through the snow on a one horse open sleigh; across the fields we go, barking all the way... woof, woof, woof!

VEGGIE PUDDING
(serves 4)

2 cups low salt chicken broth
3 cups chopped carrots
1 1/2 cups frozen peas, defrosted
1/2 cup low-fat milk
2 tablespoons wheat germ
1 cup cooked brown rice

Preheat oven to 350 degrees.

Cook carrots in chicken broth until tender. Drain and save 1 cup of liquid. In a food processor or blender, blend carrots, 1/2 cup milk, and the cup of the saved chicken broth until smooth. Add brown rice, wheat germ and whole peas. Spoon into lightly greased baking dish. Bake uncovered for 30 minutes.

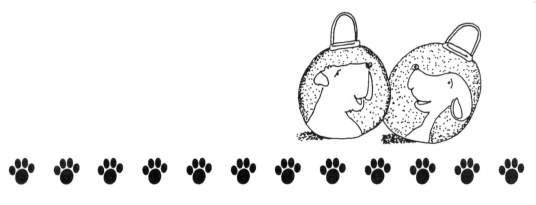

CHICKEN POT PIE WITHOUT THE CRUST
(serves 4)

1 whole chicken, deboned cut into bite size pieces
1 small onion, chopped
2 tablespoons butter or margarine
3 tablespoons flour
2 cups low salt chicken broth
1 bay leaf
1 1/4 teaspoons dried tarragon leaves

Brown chicken pieces with onions in a Dutch Oven or large saucepan. Blend flour with 1/4 cup broth . Add to chicken with a bay leaf and the remaining chicken broth. Cover and simmer for 30 minutes. Add tarragon and cook for 5 more minutes. Serve at room temperature. Leftovers can be frozen for your next dinner.

DID SOMEONE SAY........

PEA SOUP
(ANDERSON'S EAT YOUR HEART OUT!)
(serves 4)

2 cups frozen peas
2 1/2 cups low salt chicken broth
1 cup cooked chicken — chunked
2 large potatoes peeled and chunked

In a small broth pot (or large sauce pan) place chicken broth and potatoes. Boil for 25 - 30 minutes or until potatoes are tender. Add peas, and cook an additional 5 minutes. Cool for 20 minutes. In a blender or food processor, blend mixture until smooth. Add chicken pieces and serve cold.

ST. NICK'S SNACK
Cookies
(3-4 dozen)

3 cups whole-wheat flour
l cup yellow corn meal
l cup rolled oats
2/3 cup nonfat dry milk
1- l/2 cups low salt chicken broth
l/2 cup corn oil
2 eggs
2 tablespoons garlic powder

GLAZE
Beat l egg . Lightly brush on cookie before baking.

Preheat oven to 350 degrees.

Mix both flours, corn meal, oatmeal, dry milk and garlic in a large bowl. Form a well in the middle of the mixture. Whisk chicken broth, corn oil and two eggs in another bowl. Stir this into flour mixture and blend until a stiff dough forms. An extra 1/4 to l/2 cup of whole wheat flour can be added if the dough is not stiff enough. Let dough rest for 20-25 minutes. Roll out dough on a floured surface, and try to keep it as thin as possible. Cut dough into shapes with your favorite cookie cutter. Brush with glaze . Bake for 25-30 minutes. Store cookies in an airtight container.

> **Even Santa would appreciate a snack that is delicious and good for him. Remember: For your four legged kids, no milk with these cookies!**

Barkmitzvah

AT A YEAR AND THREE QUARTERS!

"BUT BOYS — YOU DON'T UNDERSTAND. YOU ARE NO LONGER PUPS, THE TIME HAS COME FOR YOU BOTH TO BE DOGS!"

CHICKEN LIVER PATE — A TRADITION!
(serves 4)

2 tablespoons butter or margarine
1/2 pound chicken livers
2 hard boiled eggs
1 small chopped onion

Heat butter or margarine in a fry pay. Saute chicken livers and onions over medium heat, stirring occasionally, for approximately 10-15 minutes until cooked through. Chop liver, onions and eggs in a food processor or blender, a little at a time. Mold into shape, and refrigerate for several hours. Serve with Garlic Snap Crackers*.

***Garlic Snap Crackers
See Page 88**

CHICKEN SOUP WITH MATZO BALLS
Max's Mother's Touch
(serves 6)

4 quarts cold water
4 pounds chicken necks, backs and legs
4 carrots, chopped
3 stalks of celery with leaves
2 onions, chopped
1 leek, chopped
1 cup parsley, chopped
2 bay leaves

Place all ingredients in 8-10 quart broth pot. Cover with cold water and bring to a boil. Reduce heat and simmer for 2 1/2 hours partially covered. When cool, strain through a colander with some cheese cloth to catch all the bones and vegetables. Place soup in container, let cool, and refrigerate overnight. The next day, the fat will have hardened on top — simply remove. Save 1/2 cup fat for the matzo balls. Soup can be frozen.

This soup is also used as chicken stock for other recipes.

For the extra special touch, add cooked boneless chicken.

MATZO BALLS

6 eggs
1 tablespoon finely chopped parsley
1 tablespoon finely chopped onion
1/2 cup chicken fat from the top of the soup
2/3 cup hot water
1 1/2 cups matzo meal

Beat eggs lightly. Add parsley, onion, chicken fat and water. Slowly add matzo meal. Mix well and refrigerate for 2 hours. Drop the mixture by the spoonful into rapidly boiling soup. Reduce heat and cook slowly for 1 hour, uncovered. Serve at room temperature.

> Remember, your four legged guests require room temperature food.

LIVER AND ONION CRISPS
(6-8 dozen crackers)

A lot of recipes throughout this book call for boiled chicken livers or boiled chicken pieces. To do this, have a large sauce pan or small broth pot full of cold water (approximately 5 cups of cold water to every pound of meat). I like to add 1 or 2 onions and a bay

(continued)

Liver and Onion Crisps *(continued)*

leaf for flavor. (The onions can later be ground up with the chicken livers, but <u>always</u> remove the bay leaf.) Bring chicken pieces or the livers to a boil, and simmer for 25-30 minutes uncovered. Drain. They can be served plain or used in other recipes. Always wait for food to cool before serving.

> 1 pound cooked chicken livers (boiled)
> 1 cup low salt beef broth
> 1 1/2 cups wheat germ
> 1 medium size onion, chopped
> 1 cup yellow corn meal
> 2 cups whole wheat flour
> 2 tablespoons brewers yeast (optional)
> Onion powder

GLAZE
Beat 1 egg . Lightly brush on cookie before baking.

Preheat oven to 350 degrees.

Using a blender or food processor, pureé the liver and onion while slowly adding beef broth. When all the liver is puréed, transfer to a large bowl. Blend in wheat germ and brewers yeast. Slowly add corn meal and whole wheat flour until the dough becomes stiff. Knead dough for 3-5 minutes and let it rest for an additional 5 minutes. On a lightly floured surface, roll the dough into a ball.

As Webster and Max like their crackers thin, I have found that the best way to do this is to split the ball into four sections and roll each section into a hot-dog shape. Wrap these in plastic wrap and chill for thirty minutes. Slice into very thin chips. Place the chips on a lightly greased cookie sheet (I always use Pam® spray when lightly greasing my cookie sheets.), and brush with glaze. Lightly sprinkle with onion powder and bake for 25-40 minutes. Halfway through, turn. As the crackers cool, they will become hard. Leftover dough can be frozen for up to 3 months.

GARLIC SNAPS
(6-8 dozen)

1 1/2 cups wheat germ
1 pound cooked boneless chicken, white and dark
1 cup low salt chicken broth
2 cups whole wheat flour (more may be needed)
2 cloves fresh peeled garlic
1 cup yellow corn meal
2 tablespoons brewers yeast (optional)
Garlic powder

GLAZE
Beat 1 egg . Lightly brush
  on cookie before baking.

> This is a real crowd pleaser. Most guests enjoy the flavor of garlic....that is, except for the fleas!

Preheat oven to 350 degrees.

In a large blender or food processor, gradually purée chicken and garlic, slowly adding chicken broth. Transfer the chicken purée into a large bowl. Mix in wheat germ and brewers yeast. Slowly adding flour and corn meal until the dough becomes stiff. Knead the dough for 3-5 minutes. Let it rest for 5-10 minutes. On a lightly floured surface, roll the dough into a ball.

As Webster and Max like their crackers thin, I have found that the best way to do this is to split the ball into four sections and roll each section into a hot-dog shape. Wrap these in plastic wrap and chill for thirty minutes. Slice into very thin chips. Place the chips on a lightly greased cookie sheet (I always use Pam® Spray when lightly greasing my cookie sheets), and brush with glaze. Lightly sprinkle with garlic powder and bake for 25-40 minutes. Halfway through, turn. As the crackers cool, they will become hard. Leftover dough can be frozen for up to 3 months.

THE SAUCY DOG

AND GRAVIES TOO!

The object of this section is to provide you with suggestions on how to avoid the waiting game. (You know...when you and your pet go nose-to-nose seeing who will give in first). Will a new brand of dog food be bought, or will your pup give in and eat kibble?

To help in this test of wills, I often add a gravy or sauce to their kibble, mixing well so they don't just eat the sauce. Adding small amounts to their regular kibble gives extra flavor without altering their diet.

CHICKEN OR BEEF BROTH GRAVY

2 cups low salt chicken or beef broth
2 tablespoons cornstarch

In a sauce pan, add the cornstarch to the broth and bring to a boil. Thicken. Serve at room temperature.

For a change, add small amounts of leftover chicken, turkey, beef or vegetables.

TURKEY GRAVY

2 tablespoons all purpose flour
2 tablespoons drippings from the roasted turkey
2 cups boiling water
1/2 cup cooked chopped giblets (optional)

Over a medium heat, blend flour and drippings to create a rue (thick paste). Slowly add boiling water while whisking until gravy thickens. Add giblets.

BARBECUE SAUCE

(For that home on the range kind of meal).

1 small green pepper — chopped
1 clove garlic — chopped
1 cup low salt tomato sauce
1/4 cup Worchestershire® sauce
1/4 cup catsup
1/4 cup brown sugar
1/4 cup red wine vinegar
1 medium onion — chopped
2 cups water

> **This sauce is wonderful with ground beef but can be used with anything.**

Combine all the ingredients together. Simmer for 30 minutes. Cool and store in an airtight container in the refrigerator.

NO BARKING AT THE TABLE

The Whooped Pooch

REMEDIES FOR WHAT AILS YOU

You'll notice that throughout this book, I have included numerous rice recipes. I have done this not only because Webster and Max love rice, but because cooked rice is especially good for firming the stool. Remember: Always check with your veterinarian when any unusual conditions are noticed. Moderation should be your guide. Too much rice can cause constipation, and you'll find yourself with a new set of problems.

Mommy, I don't feel good.......

A little bit of rice goes a long way.

BOILED BURGER
(serves 2)

1 pound ground beef
6-8 cups water

In a large sauce pan or small broth pot, bring water to a boil. Add meat, breaking it up as you add to water. Boil for 15-20 minutes until cooked through. Drain in a colander and rinse well. Cool and serve with plain boiled rice.

PLAIN BOILED RICE

(serves 4)

1 cup long grain white rice
2 cups water

In a sauce pan, bring water to a boil. Add rice and stir. Turn stove down and cover rice. Simmer for 20 minutes. Remove from heat and keep covered for an additional 5 minutes. Cool, and serve plain or with boiled hamburger.

HINTS

Ice cubes are especially helpful for the teething puppy. Most enjoy the coldness in their mouth, plus it helps the aching gums. Take a clean rag and wrap ice cubes inside. This can be a fun and healthy toy to be played with outdoors.

Giving your dog medication can be a real pill, but it doesn't have to be a problem. Here's a trick we use at our house. I bury the pill in a treat and begin praising Webster like I normally would before giving him something special. Then I pop the treat in his mouth and we're done. The best camouflage material is a piece of cheese, soft white bread rolled into a small ball or his favorite, chunky peanut butter. Note: Be sure to confirm with your veterinarian that the pill can be given with food.

NO BARKING AT THE TABLE

ADD YOUR OWN RECIPES

CANINE RECIPES MOST BEGGED FOR

ADD YOUR OWN RECIPES

NO BARKING AT THE TABLE

ADD YOUR OWN RECIPES

CANINE RECIPES MOST BEGGED FOR

ADD YOUR OWN RECIPES

NO BARKING AT THE TABLE

ADD YOUR OWN RECIPES

CONVERSION TABLES

LIQUID MEASURES

American Cup	Imperial Cup
1/4 cup	4 tablespoons
1/3 cup	5 tablespoons
1/2 cup	8 tablespoons
2/3 cup	1/4 pint
3/4 cup	1/4 pint + 2 tablespoons
1 cup	1/4 pint + 6 tablespoons
1 1/4 cups	1/2 pint
1 1/2 cups	1/2 pint + 4 tablespoons
2 cups	3/4 pint
2 1/2 cups	1 pint
3 cups	1 1/2 pints
4 cups	1 1/2 pints + 4 tablespoons
5 cups	2 pints

SOLID MEASURES

	American Cup	Imperial Cup
Butter	1 tablespoon	1/2 ounce
	1/4 cup	2 ounces
	1/2 cup	4 ounces
	1 cup	8 ounces
Cheese (grated)	1/2 cup	2 ounces
Cornmeal	1 cup	6 ounces
Flour	1/4 cup	1 1/4 ounces
	1/2 cup	2 1/2 ounces
	1 cup	5 ounces
	1 1/2 cups	7 1/2 ounces
	2 cups	10 ounces
Herbs	1/4 cup	1/4 ounce

(continued)

SOLID MEASURES *(continued)*

	American Cup	Imperial Cup
Sugar	1/4 cup	1 3/4 ounces
	1/2 cup	3 ounces
	1 cup	6 1/2 ounces
Vegetables	1/2 cup	2 ounces
	1 cup	4 ounces
Wheat Germ	1/2 cup	1 1/2 ounces
	1 cup	3 ounces

OVEN TEMPERATURES

	°F	Gas Mark	°C
Cool	225-250	1/4-1/2	110-120
Very Slow	250-275	1/2-1	120-140
Slow	275-300	1-2	140-150
Very Moderate	300-350	2-3	150-160
Moderate	375	4	180
Modertely Hot	400	5-6	190-200
Hot	425-450	7-8	220-230
Very Hot	450-475	8-9	230-240

INGREDIENT NAMES

All-purpose flour	=	Plain flour
Brown sugar	=	Soft brown sugar
Baking soda	=	Bicarbonate of soda
Molasses	=	Treacle

SEND US YOUR RECIPES

Please send us your suggestions for healthy recipes.

If there is a lipsmacking response, we will include these — with your permission — in our next book.

Lip Smackers, Inc.
P. O. Box 5385
Culver City, CA 90231-5385

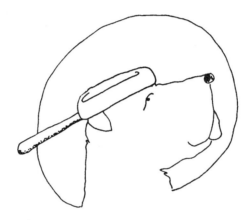

Index

LAMB:

Nuthin' but mutton (and veggie) stew, 40

PORK:

Quiche lorraine for the bacon and egg lover, 22

Prosciutto with cheese sticks, 24

Maureen's green eggs, 34

So why do they call them scotch eggs, 39

RICE:

Meatball cocktail, 21

Rice for the true rice lover, 28

A loaf with some real spring, 41

Spinach rice, 45

A brown rice fit to be fed, 49

Chilly chicken rice supreme, 59

Bethann's carrot rice, 60

Paula T's rice, 65

Fried rice, 70

Mushroom and cheese rice, 76

Veggie pudding, 78

Plain boiled rice, 95

TUNA:

Tuna pate, 25

Tuna delight with a broccoli bite, 44

TURKEY:

Turkey cutlets, 46

Bird in a pan, 74

VEGETABLES:

Half baked broccoli, 35

Green and mean zucchini casserole, 36

A loaf with some real spring, 41

Tuna delight with a broccoli bite, 44

Spinach rice, 45

Your pooch will love these "pasta-bilities", 55

Bethann's carrot rice, 60

Low-cal grilled vegetables for the barbe-cue, 69

Chicken loaf, 75

Zucchini pancakes, 75

Mushroom and cheese rice, 76

Veggie pudding, 78

Pea soup, 80